ChurchBusters:
The Men Who Will Destroy Your Ministry and The Spirits that Will Destroy the Men

A Tale of Two Kings
("Excellence in Ministry")

A Study of the Idolatry of Kings Asa and Jehoash

Fifth Edition January 2024
Copyright © 1996, 2019 by Dr. Steven A Wylie
All Rights Reserved Worldwide

AUTHOR'S NOTE

Throughout this episode the term "man" is used to describe a character who is a "male" as well as an order of creation known as "man-faced" which includes both genders of male and female characters.

Dedication

To All of Those Who Want

All that the Lord Has for Them

and

Who Want to Be All That They Can Be

In the Kingdom of Our God!

Kingdom Principles Presented in this Episode

- **Kingdom Principle:** You can remove the people from the high places, but you can't always remove the high places from the people.

- **Kingdom Principle:** We lead by serving and we serve by leading.

- **Kingdom Principle:** That which is upon the head will always flow down to cover the body.

- **Kingdom Principle:** It is better to please the LORD than to please the people. Ask Saul.

- **Kingdom Principle:** You won't get rid of the cobwebs until you get rid of the spiders.

- **Kingdom Principle:** We can decide for ourselves but we are not going to be able to control the choices of others.

- **Kingdom Principle:** Don't beat the messenger just because you don't like the message.

- **Kingdom Principle:** The way we leave is the way we enter, and the way we enter is determined by the way we left.

- **Kingdom Principle:** Go to God about the people before you go to the people about God.

- ❖ **Kingdom Principle:** The ends do NOT justify the means.

- ❖ **Kingdom Principle:** The LORD is looking for men of Convictions instead of men with Preferences.

- ❖ **Kingdom Principle:** Go to the LORD to Get Clean to Stay Clean.

- ❖ **Kingdom Principle:** It is easier to "obtain" than it is to "maintain."

Topics Discussed
In This Episode

- ✓ **PREFACE**

- ✓ **WHO WAS THIS KING ASA?**

- ✓ **CONSECRATION AND DEDICATION STARTS AT THE TOP**

- ✓ **WHEN PEOPLE TRUST**

- ✓ **THE BLESSINGS OF FAITH**

- ✓ **A TIME OF GREAT MINISTRY**

- ✓ **INFLUENCE INCREASED**

- ✓ **OPPOSITION OF FAMILY TRADITIONS**

- ✓ **COMING TO PEACE WITH REMNANTS**

- ✓ **INTERVENTION OF INTERFERENCE?**

- ✓ **MEANS TO AN END**

- ✓ **RUN TO FINISH THE RACE**

- ✓ **WHO WAS THIS KING JEHOASH?**
- ✓ **PRIESTS AND KINGS**
- ✓ **ONLY ONE GOD**
- ✓ **CONVICTIONS OF PREFERENCES**
- ✓ **HOW THE MIGHTY FALL**
- ✓ **INDENTIFYING IDOLS**
- ✓ **GOOD – THE ENEMY OF BEST**
- ✓ **CHURCHBUSTERS**
- ✓ **YOU ARE A ROYAL PRIESTHOOD**
- ✓ **THERE IS ALWAYS A CHOICE**
- ✓ **SOLUTION: HOW TO REMOVE THE HIGH PLACES AND IDOLS**
- ✓ **THE RESULTS OF SINS BEING CONFESSED AND RENOUNCED**
- ✓ **HIGH PLACES, THE OCCULT AND ALL FORMS OF IDOLATRY**
- ✓ **ACCURSED OBJECTS IN THE HOME**

- ✓ **ALL THINGS CONSIDERED**

- ✓ **FROM THE AUTHOR**

- ✓ **MY STUDY NOTES**

ChurchBusters:
The Men Who Will Destroy Your Ministry and The Spirits That Will Destroy The Men !!!

SEASON ONE INTRODUCTION

❖ **Kingdom Principle:** Every Ministry has a Prison but every Prison has a Key to unlock it.

We know that the things that God has given us in His Word record the good and the bad, the strengths and the weakness of men and women in the Bible. We know that they are accurately recorded that we may learn from what others have done.

We can learn from the good that someone does as well as from the bad that they do. We need to emulate and follow after their good examples as well as to remember not to emulate and follow their bad examples.

❖ **Kingdom Principle:** Find out what works, and do more of it!

❖ **Kingdom Principle:** Find out what doesn't work, stop doing it immediately, and never do it again!

There are 14 episodes in Season One of "ChurchBusters". While each episode will build off of the preceding episode's lessons and kingdom principles, every episode is a "stand-alone" study lesson worthy of individual attention and consideration. You may dive in at any point of Season One and not wonder if you missed out on anything.

You will discover "Kingdom Principles" throughout "ChurchBusters" that will illustrate the examples and will help you to understand the Word of God in a deeper and richer way.

Why should we keep re-inventing the wheel? It has been proven time and time again that the wheel works best when it is round. It doesn't matter how big it is, only that it works best when it is round.

When we read the Bible we learn that we should do what works, and do more of it, and when we discover what does not work stop it immediately, and never do it again!

"ChurchBusters" is directed towards the pastors of Churches and to the leaders of ministries, both "great and small". It is also written for both new Christians as well as the seasoned, mature Believers and will hopefully encourage them to further study the Word of God. For the unbeliever or "un-Churched" it may be an eye-opening series of episodes that will draw them closer to Jesus.

Its direct, hard hitting, "right between the eyes" style is a "no punches pulled" for men and women of God who desire to improve their walk and relationship with the Risen Christ. It is written to these unique individuals who are willing to take a closer look at their lives and do a "reality check".

At times, "ChurchBusters" will be instructional, and at other times it will be correctional. It will cause these men and women to look into the hearts of those that God has placed around them in their ministries and in their congregations.

Sometimes it is going to be directed at those of you who are in a "servant's position" in the Church. See if there is a tugging and conviction on your heart that maybe things are not quite the way that they should be.

But fair game and fair warning! What "ChurchBusters" will be speaking to the pastors about the church will cause them be looking at you in perhaps a new light, and what it reveals to the Body of Christ will cause them to look at those in leadership in perhaps a different light as well.

It is a close self-examination. It is not intended to be a criticism of any particular person or ministry or Church. It is intended to pull out the examples that God has given us in His Word so that we can profit from them and then grow by these examples. It is not intended to point fingers or try to "fix the blame". There is more than enough blame in the Church to go around without pointing fingers outwardly.

"Blessed are the peacemakers, they are God's children, let peace begin with me". So, if you find someone you know, your brother or your sister, closely identifying with either the men or the spirits behind the examples, remember ... "let peace begin with me".

With every example that God gives us we can learn from the good and the bad. We are going to be looking at the some of these men and the spirits that destroyed them because these are present in today's Church. Just like the "wheat and the tare" grow up in the field together, in the Church you are going to find the genuine and the counterfeit.

You will learn how to differentiate between a sheep and a goat and to discern which are friendly sheep and which are unfriendly sheep, and which ones are goats and which ones are wolves!

Don't be deceived, by their fruits they shall be known.

You are going to find these men who destroy ministries and the spirits that destroy these men in your own midst, even within your own congregation. And you are going to find them outside the walls of your church, just like when Nehemiah encountered Sanballot and Tobias in the Valley of Ono.

You are going to find them in authority over you as well as under your authority. You will see what happened to them and understand how to deal with them when you encounter them.

Remember that this is not intended as a negative criticism of any person, their kingdom, their rule, their reign, their life, or their ministry. It is simply about the men that will destroy your ministry and the spirits that will destroy the men.

Episode 8

A Tale of Two Kings
"Excellence in Ministry"

A Study of Idolatry of King Asa and King Jehoash
2 Chronicles 14:2-3 • 2 Kings 12:2-3

Idolatry: That on which the affections are passionately set; Something that occupies the place, time or affections Due a Holy God.

ChurchBuster Spirit:

- ✓ Spirit of Idolatry
- ✓ Spirit of Man-Fear
- ✓ Spirit of Disobedience

Preface

Serving in ministry in any capacity takes guts. When one assumes the role of leader within a church they in essence put a target on their back – a spiritual one and a physical one.

Whether warranted or not, ministers and church leaders are held to a higher standard than others and perhaps they should live at a higher standard as by default they are the example many look to emulate in their desire to know God more.

One of the greatest ChurchBusters is "idolatry". I'm not talking about eight foot tall totem poles of carved birds and beasts standing in the corner of our living rooms. I'm talking about anything that comes between us and the relationship that God desires to have with us.

In Scripture are two kings that exemplify what happens when good men and women fail to remove idols from their lives and the impact these idols can have on their ministries and the lives of those under their ministry.

These two kings were King Asa and King Jehoash.

Both men were said to be good men who "did what was right in the eyes of the Lord" but beyond that there was a significant difference between the two.

Here is their ChurchBuster episode.

Who Was This King Asa?

In 2 Chronicles 14 we are introduced to King Asa. He was the son of King Abijah and Asa took over the throne when his father died. We are told that during the first ten years of his reign his land was quiet. There was no war. It was a time of peace. During this time King Asa did something remarkable:

> *"Asa did that which was good and right in the eyes of the Lord his God.*
>
> *"For he took away the altars of the strange gods, and the high places, and tore down the images, and cut down the groves: And commanded Judah to seek the* LORD *God of their fathers, and to do the law and the commandment."*
>
> *"Also he took away out of all the cities of Judah the high places and the images: and the kingdom was quiet before him."* (2 Chronicles 14:2-5)

These high places and groves were filled with people. Trees represent "people" and groves represent a lot of people in one location. "High places" are those things that have a strong hold on the people's hearts and minds.

- ❖ **Kingdom Principle:** You can remove the people from the high places, but you can't always remove the high places from the people.

King Asa removed the altars. He removed the high places or the raised altars set aside for idol worship. He destroyed the carved images and statues, also known as Asherah poles.

He cut down the groves which were places that were set aside for the specific purpose of sexual cult rituals in worship of the fertility goddess, Asherah, who was said to be the wife or companion of the god Ba'al and of, some even claim, Yahweh, or God.

The entire city of Judah was freed from idolatry.

King Asa knew that the worship of idols was not following the designs of God and that the practice of these fertility rituals and cult rites had absolutely nothing to do with the worship of God. As king, he insisted that his people seek the God of their fathers, not some hybrid feel-good god that had been piece-worked from multiple religions and social preferences.

He told them to go back to the practice of the law and the commandments that God gave Moses and the Israelite people. King Asa knew that if his people followed his directive and removed all of the idols from their lives that there would be peace in their lives, in their hearts and in their kingdom. He knew that idol worship was a ChurchBuster, or in his case, a Kingdom Buster.

Consecration and Dedication Starts at the Top

- ❖ **Kingdom Principle:** We lead by serving and we serve by leading.

He wanted better for his people and he set this example. He led his people in a path of honoring and worshipping God consistently, faithfully and blamelessly.

We are told that during this time of peace that they built fences. Fences have the dual purpose of keeping people out and keeping people in. Enemies were kept out and communities were knit together in peace and security.

Fences also establish boundaries and possession. During this time they staked claim where they were at. They claimed the land that the Lord God had given them. They lived mightily within their inheritance through God.

We are told that they built and prospered and that the Lord gave them rest. They were able to do their work without interference. They grew and their mission and their influence grew with them all because their king had said, "No more idols, we will only serve God."

- ❖ **Kingdom Principle:** That which is upon the head will always flow down to cover the body.

As the anointing oil was poured out upon Aaron's head, it flowed from his head to his shoulders, down his arms and finally on to the soil around him – soil can represent mankind or the people around us.

If our "covering" is holy then our lives will be holy, but if the covering over us is in sin then we are open to be influenced by that sin(s).

Pastors who have a heart for the lost will have people in their church who are likewise driven to go seek and find the lost.

Pastors with sex sin issues or integrity issues put their Church in danger with those sins affecting the lives of the families.

When People Trust

Between the tribes of Judah and Benjamin, we are told that King Asa had 580,000 "mighty men of valor". Imagine what can be accomplished with 580,000 men fearless in their pursuit of serving God!

When the Ethiopian army of "a thousand thousand" or one million soldiers came against King Asa's army they didn't know what they were in for. King Asa didn't rely on his mighty men of valor, instead, he turned immediately to God.

> *"And Asa cried unto the LORD his God, and said, LORD, it is nothing with thee to help, whether with many or with them that have no power: help us, O LORD our God; for we rest on thee, and in thy name we go against this multitude. O LORD, thou art our God; let no man prevail against thee."* (v.11)

Think about what would happen if, as leaders when faced with problems, instead of relying on our Mighty Men and Women of God we first turn to God and say, "God, for You to give Your help in this situation is easy. It doesn't matter if we face a big problem or a small problem; we put our trust in You. You are our God. Protect us."

> *"Some trust in chariots, some in horses but we will remember the Name of the Lord our God."*
> (Psalms 20:7)

Don't put your trust in your money or your men. To do so is to return to your idols. Leaning on your reputation, your position, your perceived personal power and your popularity are other examples of modern day idol worship.

God would hear us just as He heard King Asa and He would deliver good results just as He came through for King Asa and his mighty men of valor. If you are dealing with the ChurchBuster of idol worship or idolatry in your ministry, turn to God. "God, it is nothing for you to give your help." Trust in God. God <u>will</u> protect you and your people.

We are told that the Lord smote the Ethiopians before Asa. God got in the battle and turned the odds in the favor of King Asa and his might men of valor. What was an almost 2:1 battle quickly became God against the million and the million quickly knew they were beat and ran.

King Asa and the men that were with him pursued the Ethiopians and they were defeated and they could not recover. We are told that the Ethiopians were "destroyed before the Lord and God's (and King Asa's) army who then carted off the spoils of war of the Ethiopians and the nearby cities.

The Blessings of Faith

Life was good for King Asa and his people. They were enjoying a mountain top experience. It was during this time of great success that a prophecy was spoken to King Asa:

> *"And the Spirit of God came upon Azariah the son of Oded:*
>
> *"And he went out to meet Asa, and said unto him, Hear ye me, Asa, and all Judah and Benjamin; The LORD is with you, while ye be with Him; and if ye seek Him, He will be found of you; but if ye forsake Him, He will forsake you.*
>
> *"Now for a long season Israel hath been without the true God, and without a teaching priest, and without law. But when they in their trouble did turn unto the LORD God of Israel, and sought Him, He was found of them.*
>
> *"And in those times there was no peace to him that went out, nor to him that came in, but great vexations were upon all the inhabitants of the countries. And nation was destroyed of nation, and city of city: for God did vex them with all adversity.*
>
> *"Be ye strong therefore, and let not your hands be*

> *weak: for your work shall be rewarded."*
> (2 Chronicles 15:1-7).

King Asa took this prophecy to heart. He wanted the peace that the generation before him did not have. He wanted a peace for his people that his father's kingdom did not bring them.

Growing up, Asa experienced no peace and he saw great vexations and much fighting. Asa wanted better for his people and he knew the only way to get that was to remove all traces of idolatry from his kingdom and worship the one true God.

And so King Asa did just that.

A Time of Great Ministry

King Asa purposed to follow God and the favour of God was upon him. People within the Judah, Benjamin, Ephraim, Manasseh and Simeon saw this and King Asa's ministry impacted them. They travelled to him to learn more about his commitment to God and we are told that they made a vow to serve only God.

> *"And when Asa heard these words, and the prophecy of Oded the prophet, he took courage, put away the abominable idols out of all the land of Judah and Benjamin, and out of the cities which he had taken from mount Ephraim, and renewed the altar of the LORD, that was before the porch of the LORD. And he gathered all Judah and Benjamin, and the strangers with them out of Ephraim and Manasseh, and out of Simeon: for they fell to him out of Israel in abundance, when they saw that the LORD his God was with him."* (2 Chronicles 15:8-9).

Asa "feared" (loved) God more than he "feared" (retaliation) of the people. He desired to be a God-pleaser instead of a man-pleaser.

❖ **Kingdom Principle:** It is better to please the LORD than to please the people. Ask King Saul.

As they gathered in Jerusalem in the 15th year of King Asa's reign, they offered sacrifices of seven hundred oxen and seven thousand sheep and "they entered into a covenant to seek the LORD God of their fathers with all their heart and with all their soul; that whosoever would not seek the LORD God of Israel should be put to death, whether small or great, whether man or woman."

With loud voices, shouting and trumpets and cornets there was such a fanfare as the entire nation of Judah rejoiced at their promise. In this mountain top experience they were together, one vision, one voice and united in their promise to seek God with all their heart and their whole desire.

They found God and we are told that God gave them rest.

Influence Increased

King Asa influenced other leaders, other ministries and other kings. Judah was at rest because the neighboring kingdom of Israel and the people of the tribes of Benjamin, Ephraim, Manasseh and Simeon were in agreement and they worked together in the worship of God.

Opposition of Family Traditions

When Azariah prophesied what he said challenged Asa. Removing the idols from his own kingdom of Judah was difficult enough but calling out the idols and challenging them in other realms was a feat that took great courage.

❖ **Kingdom Principle:** You won't get rid of the cobwebs until you get rid of the spiders.

Removing idolatry wasn't easy. In fact, there was a tough call to be made because idolatry was so entrenched within his own family that King Asa had to remove his own mother, Maachah, as queen because she made an idol in a grove.

We are told that King Asa cut down her idol, stamped it and burned the idol at the brook Kidron. This place, Kidron, was a transitional place throughout scripture. David crossed it while running away from Absalom, Jesus crossed it right before He was betrayed by Judas and it was at Kidron that idols were destroyed.

This dark, gloomy place was a place of dishevelment where lives were turned upside down and the old ways forsaken and people walked away from Kidron changed and made new.

> *"And also concerning Maachah the mother of Asa the king, he removed her from being queen, because she had made an idol in a grove: and Asa cut down her idol, and stamped it, and burnt it at the brook Kidron."* (2 Chronicles 15:16)

King Asa got rid of anything in his kingdom that competed with God. He showed us that the high places in our lives can be swiftly and severely destroyed. We have the power and authority in Christ to remove from our lives anything that displaces and displeases God.

He moved with courage and conviction even inside of his own family, making difficult decisions out of love and for the purpose of heaping blessing, not curses, upon his family.

If in the same situation, what would our decision be? Would we have the courage to swiftly and severely remove the obstacles that keep us from a growing relationship with God?

Coming to Peace with Remnants

The fervency of King Asa impacted not only the nation of Judah but also those with the Kingdom of Israel, Judah's northern neighbor.

One can only imagine the sense of relief as the Spirit of God moved among the people and united them in a ministry that would span multiple nations.

It would be tempting for Asa at this point to want to doggedly pursue any traces of idolatry and swiftly and severely remove those idols.

While there was a time and a place for idols to be removed within one's sphere of influence, life did not always work like that for King Asa nor does it work that way for us.

We often have to come to peace with remnants of idolatry left in the lives of others and not let it ruin the work God is doing.

God changes hearts and He is in control. We need to make sure that our relationships are grace-filled and reflect that truth.

Intervention or Interference?

King Asa's work was to follow the teachings of God and uproot any idols inside his own life, his family's life and inside of his sphere of influence.

There came a point where King Asa's sphere of influence overlapped with another prominent leader's sphere of influence.

At this place, it was up to the other king or leader to further the influence King Asa infused into his life and listen to God's voice speaking in his life.

We are told in verse 17 that "the high places were not taken away out of Israel: nevertheless the heart of Asa was perfect all his days."

In spite of all of the promises, in spite of all of the flooding of the Spirit of God in their shared mountain top experience and in spite of all that God had done to work through them and in them, the King of Israel still held on to his own "high places".

He held on to the one thing King Asa knew he had to destroy for Judah.

- ❖ **Kingdom Principle:** We can decide for ourselves but we are not going to be able to control the choices of others.

Control and manipulation is witchcraft. At some time we may have to make the decision to release those who will not come in to alignment with holiness, even though they may be very near and dear to us.

We must allow them their personal choices, just as God allows us ours.

Although we may believe and God may give us a revelation that one decision is better than another, God designed each of us with the ability to choose.

We have to come to peace with that or we will hinder God's work. Ultimately, God is the judge, not us.

Like Asa, we can keep our heart focused on God in spite of what others do or do not do or what others say or do not say. We can purpose to be perfectly devoted to God for our lives. God is our judge.

Means to an End

From the 15th year to the 35th year there was peace in King Asa's kingdom. He had 20 years of phenomenal and blessed ministry. God gave them rest and they were able to build and work in incredible ways without hindrance.

In the 36th year, things changed. Baasha, the King of Israel, the same king who did not remove the high places in Israel 20 years before, decided to build a fortified city, Ramah, for the purpose of preventing the people from coming either from Judah or going to Judah.

We aren't told Baasha's reasons or what motivated him to break two decades of peace and interfere with two decades of ministry and work to destroy it, we are only told that he choose at this point and time to stop working with King Asa and start working against him.

Business as usual stopped for King Asa and his people. Their livelihood and trade was stopped by King Baasha.

King Asa could have turned to God and had God fight his battles for him. He had witnessed how God had defeated the Ethiopian army that outnumbered his men 2 to 1. But this time he didn't do that.

In less than 20 years, King Asa forgot how ineffective he was without the blessing of God on his life.

Instead of turning to God, he took gold and silver and treasure from the house of God and sent it to Benhadad, a neighboring king in Syria.

King Asa reminded him of the treaty between their two kingdoms that went back for generations. He wanted the other king to fight his battle for him. He instructed the other king to break his treaty with the King of Israel and fight for him.

The King of Syria goes on to fight the people of Israel, making his way to the border town of Ramah to fight King Baasha. King Benhadad of Syria defeats Ijon, and Dan, and Abelmaim, and all the store cities of Naphtali. King Baasha gets word of what is happening and he knows he is next. Instead of sticking around, he and his people run and abandon the work they had started.

It seems that King Asa's tactic worked. King Baasha was no longer a threat. However, Hanani the seer came to King Asa and told him exactly what he had done. Hanani showed King Asa the big picture.

> *"Because thou hast relied on the king of Syria, and not relied on the LORD thy God, therefore is the host of the king of Syria escaped out of thine hand.*
>
> *"Were not the Ethiopians and the Lubims a huge host, with very many chariots and horsemen? Yet, because thou didst rely on the LORD, He delivered them into thine hand.*
>
> *"For the eyes of the LORD run to and fro throughout the whole earth, to shew Himself strong in the behalf of them whose heart is perfect toward Him.*
>
> *"Herein thou hast done foolishly: therefore from henceforth thou shalt have wars."* (2 Chronicles 16:7-9)

In effect, Hanani said, "You messed up. Wow, did you ever mess up. Because you did not have God fight your battles for you – the same God who defeated the Ethiopians and the Lubims – a huge army if you recall – you really did it now. God isn't blind. He saw what you did and because of your reliance on the King of Syria, your best buddy just became your worst nightmare."

Because King Asa did not rely on God, he not only relied on King Benhadad but also funded Benhadad's entire military Operations and he cleared the way for the King of Syria to come right to his door and fight him and his people.

> *(Author's Note: Isn't this the very same thing that our national leadership has been doing for decades? Setting up puppet dictators to do the dirty work and then later realizing that they have become our enemies and we depose them with yet another puppet dictator?*
>
> *(The cause and effect are the same ... and I suspect that the reason that they have done this is exactly the same reason that Asa did it ... failure to rely and trust in God and rely on self instead ... it would not surprise me if Asa had some buddies around him that made money off of his decision to fund and arm Benhadad's army.)*

- ❖ **Kingdom Principle:** Don't beat the messenger just because you don't like the message.

King Asa did not like what Hanani had to say and he took his frustration out on the messenger and threw him in jail and we are told that he also took his frustration out on "some of the people" at the same time.

Instead of owning up to his mistake, King Asa placed the blame on others. Instead of admitting that he had forgotten how much he needed God and that he needed to depend on God to fight his battles for him, King Asa was obstinate and prideful.

He had forgotten that it was God who had built his ministry, not himself. It was God who had brought peace to Judah because of King Asa's obedience. King Asa had not done that. God had.

In his final years, King Asa did not finish well. In the 39th year of his
reign as king we are told that King Asa began to have a disease in his feet. We are not sure what this disease was and can only speculate.

What we do know is that his foot disease got worse and instead of relying on God to heal him we told in Scripture that Asa turned to the physicians.

- ❖ **Kingdom Principle:** The way we leave is the way we enter, and the way we enter is determined by the way we left.

When we turn "to" something we are turning "from" something else. By design, a man cannot go "to" something without coming "from" something else. It makes the choice very simple.

Serve God or serve man.

> *"And Asa in the thirty and ninth year of his reign was diseased in his feet, until his disease was exceeding great: yet in his disease he sought not to the LORD, but to the physicians."* (2 Chronicles 16:12)

Run the Race to Finish

Asa started off his ministry on fire. The Spirit of God moved mightily in him and his people saw and experienced the blessing that peace brings for nearly two decades.

In the end, King Asa forgot that it was God who gave him strength and it was God who brought the success to his ministry. Asa began to rely on his own abilities to solve problems instead of trusting God and the end result cost him.

This was a ChurchBuster.

Anything that occupies our time, talent or treasuries can become our personal idol.

It can be our friends, our family or our finances. It can be prestige, status, appearances or positions. It can be worries about what others might think if they knew the truth.

Pornography's root cause lies in idolatry.

When pornography's roots take hold our time and our thoughts are given over to it, and while most would not call it "worship" the hold that it has on us is taking away from the hold that the Spirit of God should have on us.

These "graven images" are burned in to our hearts and minds, occupying the place where our Holy God desires to reside.

And just as the desire to seek more of Jesus pulls us to Him, if that space in our lives is filled with sin, then that sin will pull us towards even more sin.

That is idolatry.

Who Was This King Jehoash?

In two chapters of the Bible we can see the ministry of King Asa unfold and we can study how he started strong and swiftly and severely removed all traces of idolatry from his kingdom.

For two decades the ministry of King Asa was strong and God was with him and blessed the work he was doing for God.

2 Kings 12 and 2 Chronicles 24 tell the story of a different king, King Johash, also known as King Joash. Like King Asa, we are told that "Jehoash did that which was right in the sight of the LORD all his days wherein Jehoiada the priest instructed him."

The reason why King Jehoash followed the instructions of the priest, Jehoiada, is that King Jehoash assumed the throne when he was seven years old. For forty years the priest, Jehoiada, served as advisor and father figure to King Jehoash.

- ❖ **Kingdom Principle:** Go to God about the people before you go to the people about God.

Priests and Kings

In these days, there were two separate "offices" that ruled and led the people. The Priests would go to God about the people and then go to the people about God.

The Kings would go to the Priests before they would go to war and the Priests would go to God for instruction and direction on behalf of the Kings. Then, the Priests would go back to the Kings about what God had said about their going to war.

As long as each of these governing entities stayed in their respective "anointing" and "calling" things remained in order. The Kings were not to lead worship and the Priests were not to go to war. Each needed the other to fulfill the duties.

In today's time we would see the Priests as the Pastors and the Kings as businessmen.

The balance sometimes gets upset but when rightly maintained the businessmen, who help fund the Pastor's work, go to the Pastor for Godly wisdom before embarking out on new business ventures, and the Pastors rely on the businessmen to bring in the resources for the work of the ministry.

As long as the boy-king went to the Priest all was well. It was when he went to the "business advisors" that his troubles began.

While priest Jehoiada lived, King Jehoash made good decisions. He did what was right in the sight of God.

He did what was right in the sight of God, <u>except</u> he did not remove the high places set aside for idols.

He served God but kept the idols and his people still worshipped gods and offered sacrifices and burned incense in ceremonies to them.

King Jehoash saw no need to sweep house. Instead he allowed the people to mix in their old ways with their new ways. This was compromise, as a result of not following the godly pattern that had been set in front of him.

This action would come back to haunt him. Holding onto the Spirit of Idolatry would be the ChurchBuster in his ministry.

Only One God

We aren't told why King Jehoash did not clear out the high places like King Asa did.

King Asa knew that there could be no other gods before God. He had removed all the traces of idols from the Kingdom of Judah and from within his home. As a result of this, for 20 years his ministry thrived.

This compromise led King Jehoash to make a faulty conclusion, which was that as long as Jehovah was the "first" God then it would be alright for the people to have their other gods "after" Him – this is twisting the words "before God" from meaning "none" or "except God" in to "after God", a fatal compromise.

He had turned in to a "man pleaser" instead of a "God pleaser". King Jehoash did not remove the high places but we are shown that it seemed good benefits would come from his reign.

2 Chronicles 14:4 tells us that Jehoash got in his mind to repair the temple. He wanted to repair what was then the equivalent of his neighborhood church. He wanted to restore glory to the house of God.

This is an honorable mission. To achieve this vision, King Jehoash instructed the priests to collect money from the people. Repair and maintenance should have been happening all along, but it had not. The king insisted that the priest go throughout Judah and Israel and collect the annual monies needed to complete the repairs on the kingdom.

We aren't told why, but the priests were slow in doing this. They did not accomplish the fundraising as King Jehoash instructed them.

The resistance from the priests might have been caused by the king's intrusion in to Temple affairs. Kings were not to rule and reign over the Church, but this king crossed the lines again.

When the people failed to respond "voluntarily" as the king had instructed the priests to tell the people, the king decided to force his actions and started collecting money directly.

- ❖ **Kingdom Principle:** The ends do not justify the means.

People, particularly Americans, "vote with their feet" meaning that they will take their presence and their finances elsewhere when they are frustrated and/or in disagreement.

If the Temple leadership had been doing their jobs properly it is likely that the people would have responded with the finances.

However, as we saw with Eli and his corrupt sons, when things are wrong in the ministry, people will vote with their feet, or in this case, by withholding their finances.
Rather than seeking God about the solutions, the priests ignored the problems while the king used his authority and influence to get his own way. And even though the work was finished, the ends do not justify the means.

Scripture is not clear on how long this request drug on unfulfilled but we are told that in the 23rd year of King Jehoash's reign that the work was not done. The Temple was still in disrepair.

King Jehoash questioned the priests, including Jehoiada, about the lack of progress. The Temple was still in ruins even after years of the priest collecting money for temple repairs.

With no real answer provided, King Jehoash stopped the priest's collections and began one of his own. He drilled a hole in the top of a trunk so that people could come and drop their money in.

As the trunk became full of funds, the King's treasurers (the accountants) counted the money and turned it over directly to the project managers who used all of it to pay the workers doing the repairs.

> *"So the workmen wrought, and the work was perfected by them, and they set the house of God in his state, and strengthened it."* (2 Chronicles 24:13)

When the workmen were done the Temple was a good as new. The restorations were made and the project completed under budget. The extra money was returned to the treasury and from these extra funds they made the special vessels needed for temple ministry.

Throughout the rest of the life of the priest Jehoiada daily sacrifices were made to God. Then Jehoiada the priest died and things changed.

Convictions or Preferences

The young King Jehoash began to listen to a different counsel from the princes of Judah. Their presentations gave a new vision to King Jehoash that included the worship of idols.

The appeal of their vision changed King Jehoash.

Instead of following the ways of God and working on Kingdom-minded work, building God's Temple and doing God's work, King Jehoash allowed himself to be swayed to return to the old ways of worshipping idols.

In the New Testament in Luke 5, Jesus spoke a parable that

outlined the events in the Old Testament story of King Jehoash.

> *"And He spake also a parable unto them; No man putteth a piece of a new garment upon an old; if otherwise, then both the new maketh a rent, and the piece that was taken out of the new agreeth not with the old.*
>
> *"And no man putteth new wine into old bottles; else the new wine will burst the bottles, and be spilled, and the bottles shall perish.*
>
> *"But new wine must be put into new bottles; and both are preserved. No man also having drunk old wine straightway desireth new: for he saith, The old is better."* (Luke 5:36-39).

It was impossible for King Jehoash to combine God's new ways with the old way of worshipping idols and expect a positive result.

Putting new wine in old bottles caused the bottles to burst and the harvest to be lost. Putting new ways inside the old model of worshipping idols was one of the ChurchBusters.

- ❖ **Kingdom Principle:** The LORD is looking for men of Convictions instead of men with Preferences.

The traditions of man, people-pleasing decisions and politicians who offer "preferences" are always going to be in direct opposition to godly men and women who live according to their "convictions".

A man or woman of God cannot be talked out of or away from their convictions, and as such as not easily controlled or changed.

> *"And they left the house of the LORD God of their*

> *fathers, and served groves and idols: and wrath came upon Judah and Jerusalem for this their trespass.*
>
> *"Yet He sent prophets to them, to bring them again unto the LORD; and they testified against them: but they would not give ear.*
>
> *"And the Spirit of God came upon Zechariah the son of Jehoiada the priest, which stood above the people, and said unto them,*
>
> *"Thus saith God, Why transgress ye the commandments of the LORD, that ye cannot prosper? Because ye have forsaken the LORD, He hath also forsaken you.*
>
> *"And they conspired against him, and stoned him with stones at the commandment of the king in the court of the house of the LORD.*
>
> *"Thus Joash the king remembered not the kindness which Jehoiada his father had done to him, but slew his son. And when he died, he said, The LORD look upon it, and require it."* (2 Chronicles 24:18-22)

Just because you do not like the message is no reason to kill the messenger!

How the Mighty Fall

In these few verses a ministry is destroyed. As the king and his people left the house of the Lord they stopped serving and worshipping God. Instead they served the groves and idols. They practiced the sexual and fertility rituals talked about in King Asa's story.

God's wrath was on Judah and Jerusalem. Yet even in His anger, God wanted to redeem His people. Then, as now, God does not desire that any should perish but that all should come to redemption.

God sent multiple prophets to them to bring them back to Him and these prophets stood up against their false beliefs but King Jehoash and his people would not listen.

The son of Jehoaida the priest, the man who was like a father to King Jehoash and would have been like a brother to the king, spoke in God's Name to King Jehoash and to the people asking them, "Why do you turn from obeying God?"

Did they not know or understand that turning away from God meant that all the prosperity they had would stop and things would stop working together for their good? In essence, when we turn away from God and bad things are going to happen.

If you forsake God; God will forsake you.

They disliked the truth he spoke – God's Truth – and they stoned him. King Jehoash instructed the people to kill Zechariah the son of the priest who was like his father. No one was safe when the king stopped listening to and following God.

Not even the king.

Later that year, a small army of Syrians came to Judah to fight King Jehoash and we are told that "the Lord delivered a very great host into their hand, because they had forsaken the Lord God of their fathers. So they executed judgment against Joash."

God allowed an enemy that He could have easily defeated to destroy the ministry of King Jehoash and leave him gravely wounded.

It was in this wounded state that the servants of King Jehoash conspired to kill him to atone for the death of Zechariah, the priest Jehoaida's son. They plotted and carried out the mission to kill King Jehoash in his bed.

The very place that should have been a place of rest and recovery became a place of death.

It was here that the vision of Jehoash to rebuild God's temple and establish a vibrant ministry ended.

Good Intentions – Poor Execution

Initially, it seemed that God had blessed King Jehoash's ministry because good things had happened. He had collected money to restore the temple and he had hired trustworthy people to make the repairs when the priests failed in this task.

He was getting the job done, but in the end all the good that he did not bear good fruit because Hazeal, the king of Aram (Syria), attacked and took all the treasures of the temple, all the sacred objects dedicated by the kings before him as well as the pieces he had dedicated.

In the end all King Jehoash's good work amounted to nothing all because he did not remove the idols and his people still worshipped idols instead of the one true God.

"To obey is better than sacrifice". Just ask King Saul.

Identifying Idols

Two kings and two very different stories.

One swiftly and severely removed the idols and all of the high places. The other held onto the remnants of idolatry and allowed the Spirit of Idolatry to permeate his kingdom and influence his people. The end result of those decisions was his own destruction.

While we may not have totems or high places in our Churches and homes, we may have idols that need to be removed just as swiftly and severely.

An idol is anything that comes between us and God. Anything that usurps our time, our talent or our treasury away from the pursuit and worship of a Most High God is Idolatry.

The Good News of the Gospel is that we have the power and authority in Christ to remove from our lives anything that displaces God.

In Churches, if leaders keep their idols and let their people keep their idols without challenge or correction – the love of money, the love of popularity, the love of position, the love of recognition, the love of power, the love of another person, or the love of a profession ... anything that is loved more than God, whether good or bad ... is Idolatry.

And the result is that there is no true fruit.

> *"Even so every good tree bringeth forth good fruit; but a corrupt tree bringeth forth evil fruit. A good tree cannot bring forth evil fruit; neither can a corrupt tree bring forth good fruit.*
>
> *Every tree that bringeth not forth good fruit is hewn down, and cast into the fire. Wherefore by their fruits ye shall know them."* (Matthew 7:17-20).

Good - The Enemy of Best

Our God is a gracious father. His relationship with us is a sure thing. He wants to bless our lives and bless our ministries but we have to follow Him, the one true God.

We cannot allow ourselves to be get sidetracked by any other love. God uses the gift of our lives and if we only give Him the remnants He can still do a good work with that but it won't be as good.

However if we give Him our lives completely and rethink the purpose of our time, our talents and our treasures then we receive the best God has to offer.

> *"Give not that which is holy unto the dogs, neither cast ye your pearls before swine, lest they trample them under their feet, and turn again and rend you.*
>
> *"Ask, and it shall be given you; seek, and ye shall find; knock, and it shall be opened unto you:*
>
> *"For every one that asketh receiveth; and he that seeketh findeth; and to him that knocketh it shall be opened.*
>
> *"Or what man is there of you, whom if his son ask bread will he give him a stone?*
>
> *"Or if he ask a fish, will he give him a serpent?*
>
> *"If ye then, being evil, know how to give good gifts unto your children, how much more shall your Father which is in heaven give good things to them that ask him?*
>
> *"Therefore all things whatsoever ye would that men should do to you, do ye even so to them: for this is the law and the prophets."* (Matthew 7:6-12)

King Asa and King Jehoash both had a choice between "good" and "best".

Both did what was right in the eyes of God but only conditionally and the measure by which they gave was revealed in the fruit of their lives.

But, while it seemed that both King Asa and King Jehoash did good things and their ministries seemed to have good fruit, neither king experienced the best that God had designed for their lives.

Both men let the ChurchBuster of Idolatry creep into their lives and displace their trust and dependence on God. They listened to their own wisdom and the counsel of others and put other things in front of the love and service to God.

The result was their ministries - by worldly standards - were good but by God's standards were not the best. In the end, neither of their ministries ever reached the level of excellence and were destroyed, never experiencing all that God had to offer.

- ❖ **Kingdom Principle:** Go to the LORD to Get Clean and to Stay Clean.

CHURCHBUSTERS:

You are a Royal Priesthood

"But ye are a chosen generation, a royal priesthood, a holy nation, a peculiar people; that ye should show forth the praises of him who hath called you out of darkness into his marvelous light." (1 Peter 2:9)

It is not without accident that we are in the ministries that we are in. God has planned every moment of our lives. He has designed every talent and He has breathed into us a spirit for ministry. He wants us wholly committed to Him.

It is not without accident that you are reading this. If God has brought you "to" this then there is something He wants to bring you "from".

There is an idol to be uprooted in your life or in the life of someone you have influence over. This idol will keep you and others from God's best in life and ministry.

If each of us will ask the question, "God, what keeps me from you?" God's answer will be swift and, yes, even severe.

Our hearts will be pierced with the bad things that are keeping us from God as well as good things.

- ❖ **Kingdom Principle:** It is easier to "obtain" than it is to "maintain."

Many of us have made positive relationships, our mission plans and even our own ministries to become idols standing in the way of our relationship with God.

We have worked hard to build up ministries and our families and our relationships for service to God but sometimes God wants us to do things differently.

It is essential in doing a good work that we frequently ask God if that work is the best work. Often, God needs to trim away good growth in order for the best growth to flourish.

There is Always a Choice

Serving God is always a choice. How we utilize our time, our talents and our treasure is all based on our choices.

We choose what we do in a day. The hours we spend on a hobby is our choice. The hours we spend watching television, surfing the internet, playing with our smart phones and tweeting and texting our friends is also our choice.

King Asa and King Jehoash and all of their people had a choice to make. They could choose to worship God or they could utilize the moments of their day worshipping the gods of sex, money, power, influence, pride and self-interest.

They had those "make or break" choices just as we do. And just like King Asa and King Jehoash, we have to choose which God we will serve.

If we choose to serve other gods and let the Spirit of Idolatry to control us, we will destroy our lives, our friendships and relationships and the effectiveness of our ministries.

If we choose to serve God, then God will bring the best to our ministries.

> *"And if it seem evil unto you to serve the LORD, choose you this day whom ye will serve; whether the gods which your fathers served that were on the other side of the flood, or the gods of the Amorites, in whose land ye dwell: but as for me and my house, we will serve the LORD."* (Joshua 24:15)

Solution: How to Remove the High Places and Idols

Seek God in deep prayer about your walk with Him and your great need of Him.

1. **Ask** God to show you what and where the idols in your life reside.
2. **Repent** of Idolatry.
3. **Renounce** each and every idol that you have been shown.
4. **Remove** each idol from your heart, your mind and your home.
5. **Rely** on God when resistance or retaliation happens.
6. **Resist** the urges or temptations to return to the familiar "groves".

The Results of Sins being Confessed and Renounced

1. **Forgiveness:** "If we confess our sins, he is faithful and just to forgive us our sins and purify us from all unrighteousness." (John 1:8-10).

2. **Mercy and Prosperity:** "He who conceals his sins does not prosper but whoever confesses and renounces them finds mercy. Blessed is the man who always fears the Lord but he who hardens his heart falls into trouble." (Proverbs 28:13-14)

3. **Deliverance and Victory in Spiritual Warfare and Restoration of Promises:** "Yet if they shall bethink themselves in the land whether they were carried captives, and repent, and make supplication unto thee in the land of them that carried them captives, praying, 'We have sinned, and have done perversely, we have committed wickedness'." (1 Kings 8:47)

High Places, the Occult and All Forms of Idolatry

High places, the occult and idolatry go hand-in-hand although you can make a god out of money, or cars, or sex and have no relation to the occult. But when there is occult activity there is always idolatry.

All occult practices entail the worshipping of other gods. Let us look at God's attitude toward the occult and the worship of other gods.

The first of the Ten Commandments given to the Israelites in Exodus 20:2-5 reads;

> *"I AM the Lord your God, you shall have no other gods before Me.*
>
> *"Thou shalt not make unto thee any graven image, or any likeness of anything that is in heaven above, or that is in the earth beneath, or that is in the water under the earth.*
>
> *"Thou shalt not bow down thyself to them, nor serve them, for I the Lord thy God am a jealous God, visiting the iniquity of the fathers on the children unto the third and fourth generation of them that hate Me."*

- ❖ **Kingdom Principle:** Idolatry (of all forms and types) takes away the covering of protection that God's blessing imparts.

Living in unconfessed and unrepentant sin is an open door to Satan's attack.

In 1 John 5:18-21, God cautions the children of Israel over and over about not serving other gods and not participating in the occult.

When the Israelites were in the desert on their way into the Promised Land the LORD commanded them in detail the things from which they should abstain in order to remain pure and undefiled:

> *"When you enter the land the Lord your God is giving you, do not learn the detestable ways of those nations there.*
> *"Let no one be found among you who makes his son or daughter pass through the fire (human sacrifice of children),*
>
> *"Who practices divination (astrology, tarot cards, Ouija board, past life readings, palm-reading, pendulum-dowsing, or any form of seeking to know the future or the unknown through intuition, or any occult means),*
>
> *"Or sorcery (the use of a drug to bring about an altered state of consciousness, or casting a spell using herbs),*
>
> *"Or one who interprets omens (an example is to see an owl in the day and say it means good luck, fortune tellers),*
>
> *"Engagers in witchcraft (mind control, manipulation, visualizations, using ones desires, will, or psychic powers to change one's environment), or casting spells (hypnosis, affirmations, decrees, chanting mantras, wazifas or "words of Power"),*
>
> *"Or who is a medium or spiritist (channeling spirits, spirit guides, consulting nature spirits, "angels", "masters", "Ascended Masters", or "Space Brothers"),*
>
> *"Or who consults the dead (in séances, or entity*

channelings).

"For all who do these things are an abomination unto the Lord; and because of these abominations the Lord thy God doth drive them out from before thee." (Deuteronomy 18:9-12).

God does not even want us to have any occult object or idol in our homes, including jewelry with occult symbols as they can be a platform for the devil to work in our lives.

Deuteronomy 7:25 and 26 commands us:

"The graven images of their gods shall ye burn with fire: Thou shalt not desire the silver or gold that is on them (no matter how much its worth) nor take it unto thee, lest thou be shared therein:

For it is an abomination into thine house, lest thou be a cursed thing like it but thou shalt utterly detest it, and thou shalt utterly abhor it, for it is a cursed thing."

Being involved with these things defiles us and causes us to be unclean before God. Seeking power or help from any other source is forbidden as we see by this command of God.

Accursed Objects in the Home

Having idols or occult objects in our home is a very serious problem today. There are plastic images of demons filling our homes in the guise of "Masters of the Universe", Dungeons and Dragons, Pokémon and countless other demonic toys and games that are open doors for the demonizing of our innocent children.

Yet, many would consider it fanatical to burn these "images of their gods with fire."

Our society is filled with symbols of ancient Babylonian sun and moon worship. Few suspect that suns and moons with faces are images of the ancient heathen gods known in the Bible as Baal and Astroth.

With the acceptance of astrology in our society there is scarcely a newspaper that does not contain a horoscope. Occult astrological signs in jewelry and on every other thing imaginable fill the stores and our homes.

Likewise, owls and frogs (spoken of as unclean creatures in the Bible), and other symbols for witchcraft are made to look cute, and are collected by unsuspecting people who don't know what these things represent in the occult.

Many Satanic symbols, worn as jewelry, are rarely recognized for what they are and become open doors for the enemy to terrorize unsuspecting lives.

Images of Mary with a halo around her head (signifying divinity) and statues of the Blessed Queen of Heaven, as she is known in the Catholic church, and in the ancient Babylonian religion is really the "goddess" Jezebel, that God loathed and reprimanded and judged Israel for worshipping in Jeremiah 44:19.

God's Word regarding having idols in their homes was not just for the Jews. He says that the children of Israel are our example that we should not lust after evil things as they did, especially, those living in the last days (1 Corinthians 10:6, 11).

Not only were idols forbidden but things dedicated to them as well.

We have a stern warning about these dedicated objects in Joshua 7 with the story of the defeat of the army of Israel because of one man disobeying God's command in Joshua 6:18 before the Israelites took Jericho:

> *"And ye likewise keep yourselves from the accursed thing, lest ye make yourselves accursed, when ye take of the accused thing, and make the camp of Israel a curse and trouble it."*

Achan did not heed God's command and during the defeat of Jericho. He took a coat, some silver coins, and a gold bar. They were not even idols but it brought a curse on the whole nation.

When Joshua fell on his face and inquired about the defeat, the LORD said that:

> *"Israel has sinned, and they have also transgressed my covenant which I commanded them: for they have taken of the accursed thing, and have also stolen, and dissembled (deceived) also, and have put it even among their own stuff.*
>
> *"Therefore the children of Israel cannot stand before their enemies, but turn their backs before their enemies, because they are accursed; neither will I be with you anymore, except ye destroy the accursed from among you.*
>
> *"There is an accursed thing in the midst of thee, O Israel: Thou canst not stand before thine enemies, until ye take away the accursed thing from among you."* (Joshua 7:11-13).

God's wrath turned away from the Israelites when they took Achan, all his family, all that he owned and the accursed thing and killed them and burnt them.

Idolatry is a deadly serious sin. It will destroy you and those around you if not repented of and forsaken.

ALL THINGS CONSIDERED:

We have written recipes for pies, cakes and cookies, and when we follow the instructions completely and use the correct ingredients in the proper amounts, we not only get the desired results but we can repeat the process and get the same results time and time again.

However, when we deviate from the recipe we will get a different result and the cake or pie will not be what was wanted or expected.

The patterns and principles given to us in the Word of God are "recipes" for success. As long as we follow the directions and use the proper ingredients in the correct amounts we will have the results that the Lord wants in our lives.

Unlike cooking and baking, when a change in the recipe might be acceptable and sometimes will give us a different taste, deviation and changing the "recipe" of the Lord will not work well for us.

Even small variations and omissions of details will have long-reaching effects.

>1. Considering what you now know the Lord requires of you, how has the omission of "small details" or changes in the recipe altered things in your life?

>2. How would you change some of the "little ingredients" that you used in the past?

3. And, how would those changes have changed the outcome for better results?

4. How do you use the Bible as your "recipe for success" in life?

Using a compass (an old-fashioned device that did not require GPS satellites, Wi-Fi or Internet access to work) for navigation, an airline pilot knows that even the slightest deviation from the set course can alter the final destination significantly.

What is seemingly a small variation in the heading, over the course of a long flight, can cause the pilot to miss the mark by hundreds, if not thousands of miles.

1. How can relying on the Word of God assure us of a "precise" destination?

2. In your own experiences, when you discovered that you were "off course", how did you re-set your directions?

3. What did you use to make your course corrections?

We know that God is Omniscient and that we have limited knowledge. He knows things that we do not. He understands things that we cannot and do not understand.

We know that He was there before we were.

We live in a society of "social media" and intense advertising and propaganda. It is nearly impossible not to be affected by the onslaught and manipulation.

1. When you look around your home, do you see things that may be are not as innocent as you once thought they were?

2. What will you do about them?

3. Once you had removed these objects, what changes did you notice in your home? In your feelings? In your life?

While it may be hard to imagine that seemingly innocent-looking objects may be "an accursed thing", we know that God sees things as they really are and not as they have been presented to us as being.

1. Do you find it hard to believe that "frogs and Pokémon" can be a point of contact to the occult?

2. Are you willing to ask the Lord to show you what "accursed objects" are in your home? In your life?

3. If there are "idols" in your life, how long should you wait before removing them?

4. What do you think the blessings might be if you remove them, even if you are not really certain that they are "accursed"?

5. What do you think might happen if you were to continue to allow them to remain in your life?

-End-

FROM THE AUTHOR

Thank you for your support. I pray that this series of Study Episodes has been a blessing to you and that you will consider leaving a positive review online. Your feedback and comments are also welcomed!

Dr. Steven A Wylie
Pastor

P.S. If You Enjoyed This Episode You Might Also Enjoy These Studies!

The Complete Episodes of ChurchBusters

Episode 1

David: The Early Years "Anointed but not yet Appointed"

A Study of the Boy Who Would Be King

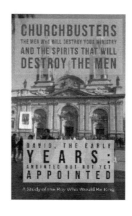

Episode 2
David: The Wilderness Years
"That Place Known as 'In-Between'"

A Study of David's Times of Preparation Before the Palace

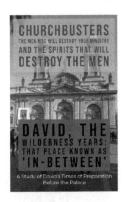

Episode 3
David: The Ministry Years, Part One

"You Can Run but You Cannot Hide!"

A Study of Hidden Agendas and Murderous Intentions

Episode 4
David: The Ministry Years, Part 2

"Follow ME and You Can Have Your Own Ministry!"

A Study of Rejection, Betrayal and Sedition

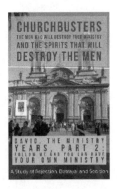

Episode 5
Moses: The Nursing Father

"Let My People Grow!"

A Study of Smothering Love and the Coming of Age

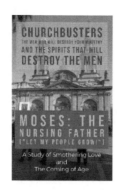

Episode 6
Samson: Power Without Purity

"A Dangerous Illusion"

A Study of God's Unrelenting Love and Loyalty

Episode 7
Eli: Justification vs. Sanctification

"If I Close My Eyes Don't You Just Disappear?"

A Study of One Father's Denials and Destruction

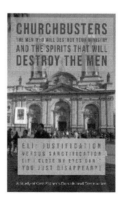

Episode 8
A Tale of Two Kings

"Excellence in Ministry"

A Study of the Idolatry of Kings Asa and Jehoash

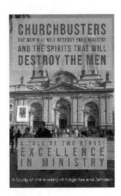

Episode 9
Nehemiah: God's Provisions

"Don't Go to Ono!"

A Study of Vision, Discouragement, Rebuilding and Courage

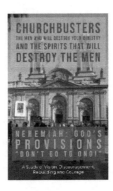

Episode 10
Jacob the Deceiver:

"He Can Talk the Talk, but Can He Walk the Walk?"

A Study of a ChurchBuster turned in to a ChurchBuilder

Episode 11
Simon the Sorcerer:

"Merchandising the Anointing"

A Study of Counterfeit, Conversion, Conviction and Community

Episode 12
Judas the Betrayer:

"Surviving the Aftermath of the Bloodbath"

A Study of Friendship, Faithfulness, Failure and Following

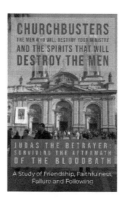

Episode 13
Jezebel and Ahab:

"He May Be the Head but I'm the Neck that Turns the Head"

A Study of Decisions, Divination, Demands and Destruction

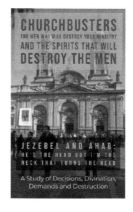

Episode 14
Moses: The Spirit of Slavery

A Study Guide of Relinquish, Release and Renewal

COPYRIGHT NOTICE

ChurchBusters:
The Men Who Will Destroy Your Ministry and The Spirits that Will Destroy the Men

Copyright © 1996, 2019 by Dr. Steven A Wylie
All rights reserved Worldwide. No part of this publication may be reproduced, distributed, or transmitted in any form or by any means, including photocopying, recording, or other electronic or mechanical methods, without the prior written permission of the publisher, except in the case of brief quotations embodied in critical reviews and certain other noncommercial uses permitted by copyright law. For permission requests, write to the publisher, addressed "Attention: Permissions Coordinator," at the address below.

Surrendered Heart Music (Publisher)
8700 West Lane Sp 167
Stockton, CA 95210
United States of America
e: Music@SurrenderedHeartMusic.com

Ordering Information:
Quantity sales. Special discounts are available on quantity purchases by corporations, associations, and others. For details, contact the publisher at the address above.

Orders by U.S. trade bookstores and wholesalers. Please contact Publisher at the above address.

Author's Note

Throughout this episode the term "man" is used to describe a character who is a "male" as well as an order of creation known as "man-faced" which includes both genders of male and female characters.

About the Author

I was born into a family lineage that included many generations of occult practitioners and evil-doers, and was the first person in my family to receive Jesus Christ. As a young child, I experienced the touch and calling of the Lord, but fell away in anger and hurt as the witchcraft and generational evils tried to destroy my life and family.

As a young boy I started playing musical instruments and writing songs, but it was not until Jesus took hold of my life (as a young adult in 1973) that it all started to flow as true music. Back then, the contemporary Christian music industry was still in its infancy and the style of worship that many Churches enjoy today was only beginning to develop but I began to express myself through the songs that I would craft and later go on to record and publish.

In high school I had two teachers that left lasting impressions on me. One was a pastor's wife who encouraged me in creative writing and expression and the other was an English teacher that I really did not like because she was hard on all of us, but especially on me (deservedly so).

She was very disciplined and strict, but I learned how to write properly and somehow, in spite of my rebellion and resistance, she instilled a love for language and communicative writing in me.

Over the years, every living member of my family has received Jesus as their Lord and Savior and is sold out to Him. Most are serving in either a pastoral position or similar ministerial capacity. Most are active in praise and worship in their own churches as well as in evangelistic outreaches.

"ChurchBusters: The Men Who Will Destroy Your Ministry and the Spirits that will Destroy the Men" was first written in 1996 but through circumstances placed on the shelf until 2013 at which time it was dusted off and editing and revisions began. Those revisions were stopped before completion that year and ChurchBusters was once again shelved.

Those revisions were completed in 2019. Each of the 14 episodes is a stand-alone study and collectively comprises the entire Season One works known as "ChurchBusters: The Men Who Will Destroy Your Ministry and the Spirits that will Destroy the Men".

Another season is in the process of being written and will be released as the Lord's timing allows.

MY STUDY NOTES:

MY STUDY NOTES:

MY STUDY NOTES:

MY STUDY NOTES:

MY STUDY NOTES:

MY STUDY NOTES:

MY STUDY NOTES:

MY STUDY NOTES:

Made in the USA
Middletown, DE
20 June 2024